Unknown
SCOTLAND
in colour

Unknown SCOTLAND
in colour

Text by
Maurice Lindsay

Photographs by
Dennis Hardley

B. T. Batsford Ltd London

First published 1984

Text © Maurice Lindsay 1984
Illustrations © Dennis Hardley 1984

ISBN 0 7134 1586 X

Printed and bound
in Hong Kong
for the Publishers
B.T. Batsford Ltd,
4 Fitzhardinge Street
London W1H 0AH

Previous page:
Ardchattan Kirk, Argyll

List of Illustrations

1

When Scotland's National Bard, Robert Burns, wrote:

O wad some Pow'r the giftie gie us
To see oursels as others see us!

he was, of course, referring to our behavioural responses, and not to the land whose contours and climate have played a major part in shaping the Scots character; what we, in fact, are as a nation. In a sense, the art of the photographer in some ways extends this power of self-survey to the physical landscape; and in an infinitely more precise manner than psychologists can record the landscape of the mind. Today, we may know Scotland in far greater detail through colour photography than was ever possible in the days when travel was difficult and stay-at-homes had to rely on the pictorial representations of painters, or, later, photography in mere black-and-white.

We Scots perhaps tend to take the beauty of our country for granted. Dennis Hardley, however, is an Englishman who fell in love with Scotland and, to the horror of his relatives and friends, in 1972 gave up a secure skilled trade in the aircraft industry to settle in Oban. Since then he has travelled the length and breadth of the country, providing many coloured covers for illustrated magazines as well as pictures for calendars, posters and other tourist publications. The sense of excitement that was to turn an Englishman from Cheshire into a Scot by adoption is evident in the sheer enjoyment which his photographs so successfully convey.

The appreciation of shape plays a considerable part in experiencing Scotland; shape, however, allied to colour and its *alter-ego*, contrast.

Land of brown heath and shaggy wood,
Land of the mountain and the flood

Sir Walter Scott called his native land. Standing time on its head, so to say, for a moment, Scott's well-known lines could aptly be capped by another line written by Burns a generation earlier:

From scenes like these old Scotia's grandeur springs.

Scotland had close ties with France from early mediaeval times. In spite of her relative isolation, however, Scotland could not escape the impact of the Norman conquest. One year after that event Margaret, the daughter of the English Prince Edward, fled to Scotland and married King Malcolm Canmore, the first sovereign to rule over a more or less united land recognisably similar in shape to modern Scotland. Saint Margaret, as she became after canonisation in 1251, rebuilt the Monastery of Iona, on the little island off the end of Mull, to which Columba had first sailed from Ireland in 563 but which had fallen on evil times during the Dark Ages. Under Margaret's two sons, Alexander I and David I, the pace of anglicisation increased, though French remained the language of the court. The French connection was further strengthened during the reigns of the earlier Stuart kings, the Auld Alliance binding Scotland and France together in mutual self-interest against England, the common enemy. That tie was formally broken in 1603 when James VI of Scotland rode triumphantly south to occupy the vacant throne of Queen Elizabeth as James I and VI, though the bond lingered on, sentimentally at least, into the early years of our own century.

Scotland welcomed occasional distinguished early travellers from

Europe; men like Aeneas Silvius, later Pope Pius II, who kept a vivid account of his visit to Scotland and the court of James I in 1435. Yet it was not until the publication of James Macpherson's pseudo-ancient Ossianic poems in 1760 that Scotland as a physical entity with a culture of her own really began to impinge upon the European consciousness. The misty glens and enormous mountains where Fingal and the Fennian heroes of Gaelic fancy acted out their vague heroic deeds, fired the imagination of those whose sensibilities had already been aroused by the romantic stirrings of *Sturm und Drang*. When Scott attracted international attention, first with *The Lady of the Lake* in 1810 and then with the long series of Waverley Novels, European travellers were stimulated to visit Scotland in increasing numbers. Suddenly, this little country seemed to embody the very essence of the romantic ideal. Indeed, Sir Walter Scott could very well be said to have been the founding father of the Scottish Tourist Industry.

It is an industry that received a further stimulus when the young and happily married Queen Victoria became fascinated by the Scottish Highlands, and in 1848 acquired a Deeside mansion at Balmoral, the granite castle which subsequently she had built for herself becoming a holiday home, as indeed it still is for her descendants. The opening up of the countryside with the spread of the railway network during the middle years of the nineteenth century made travelling possible for ordinary people, and not just for the landed gentry increasingly intent upon acquiring vast tracts of the Highlands as shooting estates, emulating the Royal example.

The coming of the automobile still further extended the possibilities of Scottish tourism. Until comparatively recently, when steeply rising fuel costs brought a check to the expansion of an industry now heavily dependent on the motorised visitor, and perhaps too vital to the Scottish economy, Scotland attracted tourists in increasing numbers, not only from Europe but also from America and beyond.

Even during the nineteenth century there developed one or two places a visit to which was regarded as essential; 'honey-pots', they are called in the jargon of those who today look after the tourist industry. The most important of these was, and still is, Edinburgh, the Capital of Scotland, which vies annually with Stratford-upon-Avon for the position of second-most-visited place in the United Kingdom after London. A desire to see Burns's place of birth first attracted Wordsworth to Scotland. The cottage at Alloway still receives many visitors, especially since the 'auld clay biggin' in which he was born on a wild January night in 1759, though long since turned into a museum, had its interest supplemented a few years ago by the construction nearby of a modern interpretation centre.

Burns, indeed, is one of the two saviours of Scotland's sense of nationhood. Through the wide-ranging nature of his poetic achievement and his great gift for drawing conclusions of universal significance from localised Scottish particulars, he not only created fine poetry shot through with easily memorable proverbial wisdom, but also awoke in the Scots a new-found pride in their Lowland tongue. He fixed in verse, too, indelible images of that age-old Scottish agrarian tradition, which had lasted more or less unchanged from mediaeval times, just as it was being assailed by the pressures of the Industrial Revolution and the genteel zealousness of the Northern Britishers wishing to annexe Scotland for themselves.

The other saviour of Scotland's sense of nationhood is Sir Walter Scott; not, of course, because of his influence on international tourism, or even because of his ability to capture the European imagination through his powers as a storyteller, important though these things were, but because of his genius in for the first time making history readable and enjoyable to large numbers of Scots people for whom previously it had been a closed, half-forgotten book. He dealt with the main confrontation points of Scottish history in the six greatest of the Waverley Novels and, contrary to common belief, invariably, if sometimes reluctantly, came down on the side of the inevitability of progress and social change. Abbotsford, 'a place to dream of, not to tell', as he himself called it, incorporates in stone his backward-looking lairdly ambitions and his enthusiastic mediaevalism through an astonishing amalgam of styles and added-on historical bits and pieces. Although he was undoubtedly a great and good man, as his *Journal* and his letters so amply testify, he was not, like Burns, directly a people's man; in no sense a radical. Thus Abbotsford, though still in the hands of his descendants and still much visited, has always yielded pride of place to Alloway in terms of tourist numbers.

'Where are we today, dear?', I once heard a blue-rinsed American lady ask her friend in a European street. 'Let's see', the friend replied: 'This is Wednesday, so we must be in Amsterdam, Miriam.' The cult of the rush-around lightning tour allows scant opportunity for the gathering in of impressions that remain. Because of its topographical conditions and its now relatively limited public transport system, Scotland is a country that demands time and leisure if it is to be allowed to yield up its unique qualities; the qualities of a small, proud nation still conscious of its isolation at the knuckle-end of Europe, still tenuously holding on to its native languages, its religion, its educational traditions, its banking system and its laws: this, too, in spite of more than 250 years of incorporated Union with England; a so-called industrial 'rationalisation' which merges countless Scottish firms into English as a preliminary to closure when the economic climate gets rough; and a physical climate that can at best be described as 'variable'.

In the pages that follow, Dennis Hardley's beautiful photographs show some of the attractions that those in search of Scotland too often miss. There are many more, of course. No one photographer, however enthusiastic, and no single album, however comprehensive, could capture the entire range of loveliness that makes us Scots cherish the natural beauty of our country, to say nothing of the variety of its man-made heritage. With the glimpse of a 'honey-pot' or two to provide, so-to-say, an anchor of familiarity, this book aims to offer the enticement and challenge of a voyage of visual exploration.

It is a voyage made possible and conducted by the seeing eye of Mr Hardley. Most of us look at things yet do not actually see them. A good photographer captures the visual moment, the substance of seeing, in much the same way as a poet captures the lyric cry. Mr Hardley is thus that comparatively rare being, a photographer whose pictures are poems for the eye.

2

It is easier to say what the Scottish scene is not than to find some all-embracing description of what it actually is. For one thing there is the divide – part geographical, part topographical, part even racial – between the Highlands and the Lowlands. This situation is further complicated by the fact that Central Scotland, where most of the 'action' takes place since almost three-quarters of the country's population of about 5¼ million people live there, differs again in character from the rolling Southern Uplands and dales of the Border country. There is also the further divide between east and west; much more than a mere matter of rainfall, though the weather in the west has links with the Highlands and what comes in across the Atlantic, while the east has drier Scandinavian-type weather appropriate to a coast that at one time felt the impact of the Norse invaders, and later developed extensive trading links across the North Sea with the Low Countries and the Hanseatic ports.

Unlike England, Scotland neither has small domestic buildings going back to mediaeval time nor obviously 'pretty' villages in the English sense of the term. Many of Scotland's most attractive villages and small towns cling round the harbours of the coast of Fife, or, like Culross, are at least within sound of the sea's moods. Others, like Dunblane and Dunkeld, cluster round a cathedral. Much of the restoration work in these places has been carried out since the Second World War by the National Trust for Scotland under its 'little houses' scheme, whereby a sum of money – originally £100,000 – was used to purchase and restore such houses to a high standard, sell them, then plough back the original expenditure and the profit into a 'revolving fund', enabling the process to begin all over again. The best of Scotland's older village houses – in the east, often harled and white-washed, with crow-stepped gables and red pantiled roofs; in the west, usually built of grey sandstone and roofed traditionally with purple-black slate from the quarries of Ballachulish or Easdale – are more severe than their English counterparts; partly, no doubt, a reflection of the colder northern clime, partly of national temperament.

Sometimes, Scotland's towns, and in all cases her big cities, developed astride or adjacent to a river. Glasgow has the Clyde, Dumfries – where Robert Burns had his final home and lies buried – has the Nith, Stirling has the Forth long before what the best of all Scottish topographical prose writers, Alexander Smith, called its 'glittering coils' find their way to Leith, the one-time independent port of Edinburgh, though since 1922 incorporated within the bounds of Scotland's Capital.

Dumfries and Stirling not only have their rivers, but also, to span them, splendid old bridges. Stirling's 'Old Brig' dates from the early fifteenth century, and that over the Nith at Dumfries is only a few decades younger. Bridges apart, though, it would be difficult to imagine two places more different in character.

Dumfries, built of red sandstone and now predominantly early nineteenth century in character, was once a prosperous sea-port serving the whole of the south west of Scotland. It is now a market town, somewhat irreverently dubbed by Burns:

Maggie by the banks o' Nith
A dame wi' pride eneuch.

Stirling has a central place in Scottish history. Its volcanic rock is

Restored 'Little Houses',
Dunkeld

crowned by a splendid once-royal castle topping a sloping mediaeval street, in some respects resembling a scaled-down version of Edinburgh. Its oldest bridge stands on the site of a wooden predecessor where, in 1297, Sir William Wallace scored a notable victory in the war against English Edward. Wallace – like Bruce, a national hero in the defence of Scotland's independence – has his valiant deeds commemorated by a Gothic-style monument, the work of J. T. Roehead, completed in 1869 on a hill overlooking the Forth Valley, and visible for miles around. In our own times Stirling has become the site of Scotland's most recent, and arguably most beautifully situated, university.

A bridge of another sort, a mere century or so old, remains one of the marvels of Victorian engineering. The Forth Railway Bridge was begun in 1882 and opened in 1890. Constructed on the cantilever principle, the central lever rests on the rock of Inchgarvie. Though this principle itself is very old – it is said to have been known to the ancient Chinese – until Sir John Fowler and his more youthful assistant, Sir Benjamin Baker, engineered this bridge no-one had dreamt of a cantilever bridge on anything like this scale. It was, and still is, a magnificent monument to the railway age, dominating the still moderately picturesque village of South Queensferry at one end and North Queensferry at the other. More than 800 years ago the inhabitants of these two places were given the right of running the ferries that preceded the bridge. The Queensferry passage – served first by rowing boat, as in Stevenson's novel *Kidnapped*, then by sail, steamboat and finally by diesel-driven ferries – finished its long history on 4 September 1964 when the Forth Road Bridge, up-river a little, was opened. It was then the largest suspension bridge in Europe.

It would be true to say that bridges, whether flung across mediaeval 'watergangs' (fords) or modern motorways, have always been among the most satisfactory achievements of Scottish builders. In a more varied and often spectacular manner the Scots have also been good at building churches, whether great cathedrals, imposing abbeys or, in later days, parish churches.

Iona holds a special place in the affections of Scottish people; not just because in its own right it is an island of great beauty set in clear waters translucently blue, but because Saint Columba landed there from Ireland in 563, thus effectively beginning the Christianisation of Scotland. Though the majority of Scots are no longer either Catholics, or even practising Presbyterian Christians, oddly enough they still vaguely approve of the religious idea and still wish their children to be inculcated in its principles.

Columba's monastery has long since disappeared. He died in 597 and in the centuries after his death Norsemen plundered and pillaged the island. Monks survived in Iona until the Reformation, though Benedictine Monks drove out the Celtic rule in Queen Margaret's time. After 1550, however, there were centuries of decay.

In July 1770, the naturalist and diarist Thomas Pennant arrived aboard a cutter of ninety tons, the *Lady Frederick Campbell*, named after the wife of his host, the ship dropping anchor 'in three fathoms of water, on a sandy white bottom'. Pennant went ashore to arrange a camping site. 'Having settled the business of our tent', he recorded, he inspected the village 'consisting . . . of about fifty houses, mostly very mean, thatched with straw of bear pulled up by the roots, and bound tight on the roof with ropes made of heath.' In the Nunnery, mostly unroofed, he found the floor 'cased some feet thick with cow-dung, the place being at present the common shelter for cattle, and the islanders . . . too lazy to remove

The Old Tolbooth, Culross, Fife

Old Stirling Brig and Wallace Monument

15

The Forth Rail Bridge from North Queensferry

this fine manure, the collections of centuries, to enrich their grounds.' In 1800, the Honourable Mrs Sarah Murray of Kensington, who wrote guide books 'to be really useful to people who may follow my steps', thought it 'a great pity that both the cathedral and the nunnery are going fast to decay. Part of the ground around the cathedral when I was in Iona was planted with potatoes and other vegetables; the rest of it was overrun with the most luxuriant weeds and wild–plants I ever beheld.'

It seems unlikely that any of the present abbey includes fragments older than the building established by Reginald, Lord of the Isles, between 1166 and 1207. There was a notable restoration during the 1870s. In 1899 the eighth Duke of Argyll gave the abbey ruins to the Church of Scotland, expressing the wish that the building might be re-roofed. By 1910, this had been accomplished. A more extensive restoration, which has included the actual monastery and other outbuildings, was the devoted work of the Iona Community, founded in 1938 by the Rev. George MacLeod, a baronet who did not take up his title but later became a life peer, Lord MacLeod of Fuinary.

Just as to those in the west of Scotland Iona has exercised the strongest hold on the pious imagination, so, in its different way, has all that is left of St Andrew's Cathedral to those in the east of the country. Once the centre of Episcopal power in Scotland the Cathedral, founded in 1160 near the older and still-surviving tower of St Regulus, took 180 years to build. Partly destroyed by fire in 1378, it was lovingly rebuilt and restored

Opposite:
The Old Bridge over the Nith, Dumfries

Overleaf:
Iona Abbey, Iona

17

St Andrews: the ruined Cathedral and St Rule's Tower

Comrie Church, Perthshire

within a century, so that its gleaming copper roof must once again have been visible far out across the North Sea. Its final destruction took a matter of hours. Following a sermon on the cleansing of the temple which John Knox preached in a nearby church in June 1559 amid

. . . . . . *steir, strabush and strife,*	(commotion)
When, bickerin fray the towns o' Fife	(quarrelling)
Great bangs of buddies, thick and rife	(gangs)
Gaed to St. Andrew's toun.	
On, wi' John Calvin i' their heids	
And hammers i' their hands, and spades,	
Dung the Cathedral down.	

That was how the event was later imagined by Anstruther-born poet William Tennant, who became a professor at St Andrew's University. Another poet, Andrew Lang, later recalled his days at Scotland's oldest university, though he went later to Oxford and thereafter spent most of his days in the journalistic purlieus of Fleet Street.

St. Andrew's by the Northern Sea,
  A haunted town it is to me!
A little city, worn and grey,
  The grey North Ocean girds it round,
And o'er the rocks and up the bay
  The long sea rollers surge and sound.
And still the thin and biting spray
  Drives down the melancholy street,
And still endure, and still decay
  Towers that the salt winds vainly beat.
Ghost-like and shadowy they stand,
  Dim mirrored in the wet sea sand . . . .

Ben Nevis from Spean Bridge

Latheron Church and Caithness coastline

Scotland's centuries-old urge to worship, however, has been marked not just by the great cathedrals and abbeys (most of them ruined, as a result either of English wars or of the iconoclasm of her own Reformers) or the large city and town churches that reflect the industrial opulence of Victorian times, many of them vital punctuation marks in our townscapes yet often struggling financially to keep going. Scottish religious feeling is also commemorated by countless pleasantly honest little village churches such as that of Comrie in Upper Strathearn, at the junction of the Earn, the Lednock and the Water of Ruchill.

It seems odd that so peaceful-seeming a place should have been subject to minor earthquakes, the first being recorded in 1789 and the worst in 1839. Mrs Sarah Murray maintained that, though 'finely situated and beautifully romantic', the ground beneath Comrie would 'one day or other open and form a lake, as the noise under ground is like the gushing of water working fresh passage through the rocks', a prophecy which, fortunately, has not materialised.

Several shocks have also occurred during the twentieth century, like their predecessors all due to the fact that Comrie sits precisely on the geological Highland 'fault'. Fortunately, nobody has ever been severely hurt and little damage has been done to buildings, facts that must more than once have drawn pious villagers to offer up thanks in their charming white-washed parish church, put up in 1804.

Other churches, like that at Latheron, in Caithness, have had no such disturbing experiences to trouble the vanished generations who now take their rest in its wind-swept churchyard. The continuity that reaches beyond religion predominates here where we are reminded of Scotland's pre-Christian past by ruined brochs, galleried dwellings, hut-circles and standing stones.

Spean Bridge, Invernessshire, lies within sight of the frequently snow-covered heights of Ben Nevis, Scotland's highest mountain. The church that was built in 1812 has associations that go back no further than August 1745. Three days before Prince Charles Edward Stuart's standard was raised at Glenfinnan, at the head of Loch Shiel, the first Jacobite skirmish

Overleaf:
Lochan Nan Druinnean,
Kilmelford

*Ben Vair and Lochan Trail
Forest, Glencoe*

29

took place near Spean Bridge. General Wade's bridge, put up in 1736 as part of the English attempt to pacify the Highlands, gave Spean Bridge its name, though Telford's bridge, build in 1819, has since carried most of the traffic.

Visitors usually come to Scotland during the months of high summer when, unless they are unlucky enough to arrive during a rainy spell, the countryside is alight with brilliant colour. Yet there is another Scotland; a Scotland whose slopes and features are transformed by snow. Like many a country church, the Kirk of Ardchattan, by Loch Etive, in Argyll, serves a scattered community. In the days before motor transport, those attending it had ample leisure to reflect on their sins during the outward journey and plenty of time to digest the sermon on the way home. Though snow does sometimes lie on the Border hills for weeks, even months, it is the Highland villages that know it best as a familiar winter companion, whether they be the remoter hamlets of the far north west, or villages relatively near the urban population like Killin, in the Perthshire Highlands.

Obviously, light and colour are interdependent. In the days before the coming of gas and electricity the fall of darkness brought with it a temporary shapeless anonymity. Even in the days of the cruizie, the tallow candle and later the oil lamp – days which carried over into the second half of the twentieth century in many parts of the Highlands – the rising light of a new day and the dying slant on an old produced changing perspectives blurred by that absence of definition which is the essence of romanticism. Such a moment is captured here pictorially, its subject the mid-Victorian parish church of Kintail, overlooking Loch Duich.

Historically, the powerful dignitaries of church and castle have tended to be natural allies down the centuries. Even today, in our multi-racial society, both the Church of England and the Church of Scotland remain established, and must be defended by Her Sovereign Majesty, though they have little real power left. Once, castles dominated the lives of the people of Scotland, giving protection and comfort to some, but all too often exercising the rigours of arbitrary bigotry and intolerance over those who disagreed with their edicts or feared their sway. The grip of castle and church has long since been broken; except, perhaps, so far as the church is concerned, in a few remote communities in the Outer Hebrides. Even there, economic circumstances and the all-pervasive influences of television on the young are forcing an inevitable slackening.

It is primarily the great glory of the natural scene, so rich in its variety, that brings people from other lands to see Scotland. They come to look upon rugged rockscapes carved into fantastic pinnacles, with caves fronting rough-browed headlands left by the retreating Ice Age and further honed by the ceaseless dialogue of the winds and the waves over countless centuries. They come to absorb distant prospects of islands across rock-fringed sandy beaches laced with marram grasses and dotted with sea pinks or yellow wild irises. They come to relax at a glimpse of rushes by a peaceful loch shore giving shelter to a fisherman's rowing boat, or white-painted inshore fishing-boats slanted at rest on shingle, the ageless symbol of man's double dependency for his basic livelihood on the fruits of the sea and the produce of the land. They come, in fact, for just those rare moments of epiphany like that caught here by Dennis Hardley's camera on the Lochan Trail Forest at Glencoe, where the turn of a season reflects the image of its dying Fall. Scotland is as rich in such moments as it is in ancient castles, sleepy harbours, and its wide variety of lochs and mountains.

A seaside rockscape near Torness, East Lothian

31

Duncansby Head, on the Pentland Firth

33

3

Most of Scotland's secular buildings possessing any antiquity are castles, a reflection not only of the country's turbulent and divided history but also of its relative poverty since, except for a few great houses, most early domestic buildings were built of impermanent materials.

Not so the castles that replaced the original wooden motte-and-bailey fortalices. Most of the older stone castles have long since vanished, destroyed by war, neglect or the elements, their fallen stones removed one by one to find their way into the walls of nearby farmhouses and cottages. Other castles lie ruined because eighteenth-century enlightenment or nineteenth-century wealth made their abandonment in favour of an unfortified but more comfortable domestic dwelling seem socially advantageous. Still others were added to, until an original tower house might almost be totally engulfed by the magpie-like stylistic eclecticism of some famous Victorian architect's romantic imagination; an imagination, incidentally, that for seventy or so years dotted the countryside with pseudo-castles and castellated mansions effulgently ornate but in late twentieth-century economic terms often difficult, if not impossible, to maintain.

Of the castles and great houses depicted in this particular collection the one whose tenuous finger-hold on time is the most precarious must surely be Castle Sinclair, erected in 1606 as a stronghold for the Earls of Caithness. It was badly damaged after an attack by a rival claimant to the earldom and deserted by the end of the seventeenth century.

Lochranza Castle, which stands on a peninsula jutting into the loch of the same name, on the island of Arran, was a royal refuge, a hunting lodge parts of which date from before 1380. It claims, indeed, connections with Robert the Bruce. James II gave it to the first Lord Montgomery, whose descendants became the Earls of Eglinton. Cromwell, that most unwelcome visitor to Scotland, stationed troops in it. In 1705 it was sold to the Hamilton family but abandoned by 1770, when Thomas Pennant's cutter arrived. He thought the approach magnificent: a bay in front, about a mile deep having a ruined castle near the lower end, on a low projecting neck of land that forms another harbour . . . . The whole is environed with a theatre of mountains.'

Another royal hunting lodge is Carrick Castle, which also stands on a sea-girt rock though in its case the waters of Loch Goil. It was a stronghold of the Lamont family, once powerful in Cowal, though for much of its active life it was in the possession of the Campbells of Ardkinglas.

Barcaldine, near the mouth of Loch Creran, four miles north of Connel Ferry, has been more fortunate. It was built towards the end of the sixteenth century by the forbears of the Breadalbane Campbells. It remained in that family's possession until, worn and abandoned, it was sold with the estate in 1842. In 1896 it was bought back by Sir Duncan Campbell, 10th of Barcaldine, who re-roofed and restored it and with whose descendants happily it still remains.

Down in the south-west corner of Galloway Castle Kennedy, built in 1607 by the fifth Earl of Cassilis, passed in 1677 to Sir John Dalrymple, the great Scots lawyer who later became Viscount Stair. Accidentally destroyed by fire in 1716 it was never re-built and now stands in the Stair of Lochinch, near Stranraer.

Another and much greater castle simply abandoned in favour of a more comfortable residence is Kilchurn, the imposing ruins of which

*The Garden at Castle Kennedy,
near Stranraer*

*Ben Lui and Kilchurn Castle,
Loch Awe*

stand on the tip of a low-lying peninsula at the head of Loch Awe, two
miles west of Dalmally. Its centre-piece is a fifteenth-century keep, once
islanded – the level of the loch has since been lowered by about ten feet,
leaving a linking passageway – but with defensive extensions forming a
substantial three-storey enlargement added in the sixteenth century and
further extended in 1693, perhaps to house the family army when Kilchurn
was still the original seat of the second most powerful branch of the
Campbells, the Lairds of Glenorchy, later Earls of Breadalbane.

After the manner of these Highland times, Sir John Campbell of
Glenorchy acquired the lands of the sixth Earl of Caithness by lending
money to that nobleman and then demanding repayment at an
inconvenient moment, an acquisition further sealed in due course by
marrying his victim's widow. During a raiding expedition to the north
in 1680 the Campbells were said to have coloured the Wick river with
the bodies of dead Sinclairs, whose lands they were seeking to annexe. It
was this story, true or false, that is said to have inspired the well-known
song 'The Campbells are Coming'. Looking at Kilchurn now, a hapless
ruin, at the height of a summer noon or in the softer hues of evening, it
is difficult to remember that it was once the impregnable seat of such
power; a centre of plotting inspired by greed and dishonesty. Dorothy

and William Wordsworth visited it in the summer of 1803, and the poet penned his 'Address to Kilchurn Castle':

Child of loud-throated war! the mountain stream
Roars in thy hearing; but thy hour of rest
Is come, and thou art silent in thy age;
Save when the wind sweeps by and sounds are caught
Ambiguous, neither wholly thine nor theirs . . . .

It is legend, however, though tinged also with cruelty, that lends the patina of poetry and romance to Cawdor Castle, about six miles south-west of Nairn. Like so many Scottish castles Cawdor developed around a simple tower, believed to date from 1396. Upper works were added in 1454 by the fifth Thane, and further extensions were added on all sides in the sixteenth and seventeenth centuries. Now, the original tall tower rises above a mainly three-storey complex embellished with angle turrets and chambers once meant to give a wide field of fire power.

Those who recall Shakespeare's *Macbeth*, and its hero's encounter with the three witches will remember the part the old title 'Thane of Cawdor' played in that marvellous tale. The first line of the family who owned the Castle was descended from Macbeth's brother. This line ended in 1498 with a daughter, Muriella. Whilst still a child and walking with her nurse she was captured by a party of Campbells. In order to make certain that she would be easily identified, with what was then thought to be great presence of mind the nurse hacked off the upper part of one of the child's small fingers. The abductor, pursued by the child's uncle, Campbell of Inverliver, inverted a huge camp kettle to make it look as if

Opposite:
Dunnottar Castle, near Stonehaven

Cawdor Castle, near Nairn

Crathes Castle, near Banchory

43

she might be concealed beneath it and ordered his six sons to defend this object to the death (which they duly did) while he escaped with his prize. In 1510 she married Sir John Campbell, a son of the second Earl of Argyll, from whom the present line descends. In spite of its relatively wind-swept position Cawdor has a colourful garden and is undoubtedly one of the best presented historic houses in Scotland open to visitors.

Dunnottar is still partly open to the winds and for long was wholly so. Dennis Hardley's swirling mists might be thought to relate symbolically not only to Scotland's present-day attitude to her national heritage and identity but also to her history, at a vital juncture of which Dunnottar played a particularly murky part. Standing on an isolated rocky promontory and pushing out into the sea a mile and a half south of Stonehaven, it was a scene of conflict even during Pictish times.

Curiously enough, it was first erected on the site of a church, a sacrilegious action which led to its builder, Sir William Keith, Great Marischal of Scotland, being for a time excommunicated. The oldest surviving section is the tall and massive early fourteenth-century keep, bell-shaped in plan and containing four main storeys. Extensive additions were built on during the sixteenth and seventeenth centuries, most of them the work of the fifth Earl Marischal, a scholar and traveller who founded Marischal College in Aberdeen.

The great Marquess of Montrose besieged Dunnottar during the Civil War. His lack of success is attributed to the machinations of the Reverend Andrew Cant, a divine whose name added a new word to the English language. After Montrose lifted the siege but wreaked vengeance on the stubborn Earl Marischal by burning most of his neighbouring property, the nobleman was informed by the divine: 'Trouble not, for the reek will be sweet-smelling in the nostrils of the Lord.'

Charles II, having signed the Solemn League and Covenant, was entertained at Dunnottar by the ninth Earl on 8 July 1650, when the king was on his way south to try to recover his father's kingdom. Dunnottar was the only castle in Scotland still flying the royal flag when in 1651 it was again besieged, this time by General Lambert. On 24 May 1652, the governor of Dunnottar, Sir George Ogilvy of Barras, surrendered; but the king's papers, which the Cromwellian general had hoped to find, had already been safely smuggled out in a body-belt worn by Anne Lindsay, a kinswoman of Ogilvy's wife. Meanwhile, the Scottish regalia – the crown, the sceptre and the sword of state – had been secretly hidden beneath the pulpit of the nearby parish church of Kinneff.

In May 1685 167 Covenanters of both sexes were packed into a small vault known as the 'Whigs Vault'. Many of them died and some of the remainder were tortured. In due course the wheel of fortune turned. Fourteen years later it was Jacobites who found themselves imprisoned in Dunnottar, this time by Viscount Dundee.

After the rising of 1715 the property and possessions of the tenth Earl Marischal were forfeited and three years later the castle was 'dismantled'. In 1925 Annie, Viscountess Cowdray, paid for consolidating repairs and some reconstruction, thus enabling the ruins of this castle, which played so striking a part in Scotland's story, to be visited in safety today.

Some castles were built for purposes other than defence in war. Long after the Union of the Crowns in 1603 and even after the Union of Parliaments in 1707 many new castles still assumed defensive postures, though in reality they were simply grand residences. One of the most handsome of these domesticated castles is Crathes, on the north bank of the Dee, three miles east of Banchory. Built in the sixteenth century as a

Balmoral Castle

44

square tower with a small projecting wing, though with later additions, it was the home of the Burnetts of Ley. It is famous for its plaster and tempera ceilings, the finest depicting the 'nine nobles', or fighting heroes of antiquity, and for a beautiful garden. Since 1951 it has been in the hands of the National Trust for Scotland, who manage on behalf of the nation several of the magnificent houses of the north east, a group which includes Midmar, Craigievar and Castle Fraser.

Also in this north-eastern corner of Scotland, now in the care of the National Trust, is Haddo House, a Palladian mansion basically the work of William Adam, built in 1731 for the family that became the Earls of Aberdeen. In our own time, thanks to the talents and energies of the Dowager Lady Aberdeen and her late husband, Haddo has become the scene of remarkable musical and dramatic activities. Famous composers and musicians have been attracted to perform or conduct there, among them Benjamin Britten and Vaughan Williams.

One castle in the north east featured in this collection is Balmoral,

Auchnacloich Castle and gardens by Loch Etive

Opposite:
Barcaldine Castle, near Benderloch

Overleaf:
Traquair House, near Innerleithen

47

which, as everyone knows, is the Highland home of Her Majesty the Queen. The history of how the young Queen Victoria fell in love with the Scottish Highlands and in 1848 bought a house originally belonging to the Earl of Fife but leased to Sir Robert Gordon is too well-known to need re-telling here. An architectural critic of the day claimed that 'the pile belonged to no recognised order and displayed no unity of design', though Queen Victoria herself described it as 'a pretty little castle in the old Scottish style'. Nevertheless, she replaced it with the present castle designed in the Scottish baronial style by William Smith of Aberdeen and built in local granite. It was still not quite finished when the Royal Family took possession of it in September 1855.

Royalty of an earlier age had connections with Traquair House, in the Borders. It stands at the junction of Quair Water and the Tweed a mile or so south of Innerleithen, and is the oldest continuously inhabited house in Scotland, parts of it so ancient that experts find it difficult to date them with certainty. A royal residence from early times, it was at Traquair that William the Lion granted the charter raising the village of Glasgow into a burgh. Mary, Queen of Scots, stayed at Traquair, and it now contains an example of her embroidery.

Gifted at various times by kings to temporary favourites, it eventually ended up in 1478 in the hands of James III's uncle, the Earl of Buchan, whose descendants became the Stuarts, Earls of Traquair. For more than a century now it has been in the hands of the Maxwell-Stuarts, coming to them through a collateral branch of the family.

Montrose called at Traquair after the Battle of Philiphaugh, but was refused admittance. Daniel Defoe, who got in, thought the house 'noble, the design great'. Prince Charles Edward Stuart also found a more hospitable reception in 1745, though he failed to win the prudent Earl of Traquair's active support. When the Prince left, the great gates were locked behind him and the vow taken that they would never be re-opened until a Stuart sat again on the British throne, a vow that has been kept to this day.

Royalty in the involuntary person of Mary, Queen of Scots, had connections with another castle, Kinross, which stands on an island in Loch Leven. Here she suffered imprisonment but managed to escape, though only to the disaster of Langside, flight to England and the long years at Fotheringhay ending with her execution, a story dramatically recreated in Sir Walter Scott's novel *The Abbot*.

Nearby Kinross House, on the mainland, finished in 1692, was built to designs by Sir William Bruce. He is really the first great identifiable Scottish architect, earlier buildings having been designed and executed by master masons, the Mylne family being reponsible for many of the royal structures. Kinross House is one of Scotland's earliest and finest domestic masterpieces and was, indeed, considered by Pennant to be 'the first good house of regular architecture in Britain'.

I have already referred to the nineteenth-century practice of dotting pseudo-castles all over Scotland, part of a cult of what George Scott-Moncrieff once dubbed 'Balmorality', a jibe which prompted Ivor Brown to retort that a mock-gothic castle set amongst the Highland hills is rather more fitting than would be a modern concrete pile.

Some of these Victorian structures, the work of great architects, are masterpieces in their own right, given our acceptance of the eclectic amalgam of styles which made up the Victorian architectural 'voice'. One such castle is Torosay, on the island of Mull, the work of David Bryce. Apart from a beautiful setting, it has the additional advantage of a colourful and well-maintained garden.

Opposite above:
Kinross House

Opposite below:
Haddo House

4

O wildly, as the bright day gleamed, I climbed the mountain's breast,
And when I to my home returned, the sun was in the west;
'Twas health and strength, 'twas life and joy, to wander freely there,
To drink at the fresh mountain stream, to breathe the mountain air.

So wrote one of the greatest of Scotland's Gaelic poets, Duncan Ban
MacIntyre, here quoted in the rather stilted Victorian English translation
of Robert Buchanan. The mountains of Scotland still exercise much the
same challenge and exercise the same sort of fascination as they did to
MacIntyre in the eighteenth century.

In some ways the most famous Scottish mountain is Ben Lomond,
since it overlooks Loch Lomond, the largest and most celebrated of
Scotland's freshwater lochs. Ben Nevis, near Fort William is, however,
the highest mountain in Scotland – indeed, in Britain – 4,406 feet above
sea level. Some Victorian climbers thought it looked rather like one
mountain piled upon another. The lower mountain seemed to them 'an
oblong mass about 3,000 feet high terminating in an alpine-like lochan',
the upper rising 'from the southern extremity of the lower . . . sloped
like a vast prism.' Two huge glens, Treig on the east, and Nevis on the
south and south west, furrow down it, and deep indentations on its other
sides separate it from the neighbouring heights. Its summit is not peaked,
but flattened, and more often than not crowned with snow and mist.

Climbing is, at best, a dangerous sport, the safety of those who practise
it largely dependent on their skill and experience. Many of those who
venture upon the Scottish mountains are quite inexperienced, unaware
of those sudden changes of weather which can turn a sunny peak into a
treacherous cloud-wrapped death-trap for the unwary, and too often
dressed in a manner more fitting for a rowing-boat excursion from an
English watering-place than the cold near the summit of a Scottish
mountain. Ben Nevis does, of course, in many respects represent the
ultimate Scottish challenge to mountaineers. Challenges and dangers
little less formidable present themselves to those who would attempt the
peaks of Skye. Blaven (or Bla Bheinn, to give it its old name), part of the
Cuillin range in Skye, occupies the upper stretch of a peninsula between
Loch Slapin and Loch Scavaig and has granite peaks with massive
shoulders that abound in crags and corries.

Most of us are quite content to look at mountains from ground level.
There are those – and I confess to being one of them – who find mountains,
like the music of the bagpipes, infinitely more poetic when mingled with
a measure of distance, like whisky with a dash of water to take out the
fire. For those of us thus field-bound, so to say, the view of Blaven across
the shores of Loch Slapin is as much a sight to remember as the less
menacing hills of Ardgour seen across Loch Linnhe. It is the prospect of
Ben Cruachan seen from Portsonachan across Loch Awe rather than the
insect-like nose-touching clutch of ascending rock-face that makes the
Highlander so sentimentally homesick when exiled to a Lowland city, or
to the larger flatnesses of England's green and pleasant land.

Glencoe holds darker memories. On a winter's night in 1691 the
Campbells treacherously murdered a sleeping party of their hosts, the
Macdonalds, in the name of King William in London. Today, it is
remembered best for the length and steepness of its valley rather than for
the heights that sheltered not only that unforgotten Campbell treachery
but, in mythic Ossianic times, Fingal and his shadowy hosts, for whom
it was the Glen of Cona.

Torosay Castle, Mull

Even in winter and from the level of us groundlings there is a kind of
ecstasy to be got from a glimpse of the high places caught in a particular
light. It was, perhaps, such a moment that inspired the Greenock-born
poet John Davidson, who became one of the Scottish associates of the
Yellow Book 'fin-de-siècle' group, to write of Strathearn –

The twinkling Earn, like a blade in the snow,
The low hills scalloped against the hill,
The high hills leaping upon the low,
And the amber wine in the cup of the sky,
With the white world creaming over the rim.

An effective and evocative description in spite of the mixture of

metaphors. In our own day Norman MacCaig, a better handler of metaphor, declared such a mountain to be 'a sort of music'.

Sheep farming in Glencoe

I listen with my eyes and see through that
Mellifluous din of shapes my masterpiece
Of masterpieces.
One sandstone chord that holds up time in space . . .

What a marvellous description of the impact great stretches of mountain make upon the human mind, evoking as it does the rousing volcanic upheaval of their creation and the great sculpting grind of the Ice Age!

Mountains are not only the delight or the playthings of man, but home for many living creatures; the deer, sometimes at a steep height seen still

Hills above Killin

Salmon nets, Portessie

Opposite:
The Cuillin Hills from Loch Slapin, Skye

and statue-like, as if scenting the dangerous air; or glimpsed bounding with a grace that arcs safety and distance; or forced by the barren snows of winter to graze in herds around the lower reaches, often within sight of busy roads.

Hill farming in Scotland is a profitable industry, and native breeds of sheep dot the lower slopes of most mountains wherever there is grass to be nibbled. Birds, too, have their haunts in the hills; especially the birds of prey, chief of which is the mighty eagle. In the Highlands and in the Lowlands it is still possible to catch sudden glimpses of age-old traditional activities; ways of life that have been carried on unchanged for centuries. By a north-east quayside the fishermen's nets will be getting repaired, often by the womenfolk; by a river estuary, as at Portessie in Morayshire, a different kind of net will be gleaned to yield the silver harvest of its salmon; or, as at Glencoe, sheep may be herded together for the shearing, or to await transport to the market.

Much emotive nonsense has been written about the Highland Clearances, which drastically reduced the population of the glens during the first half of the nineteenth century. While changing standards of living would have made it impossible for many a glen and strath to support at an acceptable level anything like the numbers content to live there in an earlier age, the appalling inhumanity of the landlords and their agents and the greedy motives which inspired their cruel actions – profitable sheep being thought more important than unprofitable humans – still form part of Scotland's inherited sense of anger. Shooting for sport later brought the leaders of British industry to the Highlands; sometimes to inhabit briefly hired shooting lodges, sometimes to buy up huge stretches of land, building mock-gothic castles or mansions, their proud owners becoming that much-despised creature the absentee landlord seen on his terrain only for a week or two during the shooting season.

There are still plenty of sheep in the Highlands and there is still shooting. Nowadays, to prevent agricultural damage and disease, that tool of natural selection, deer have to be culled and wilderness areas 'managed'. The Nature Conservancy undertake this task, as also in some cases do the National Trust for Scotland. The object, of course, is to ensure that ruthless man, the greatest predator of all, does not further desecrate or destroy the little that is left of those wild and lonely places where the human spirit can find peace and restoration, and which, in the tightly packed Britain of today, are now almost all located in the Highlands and Islands of Scotland.

5

It is difficult to imagine Scotland before the railway era, served and supplied by innumerable small ports strung out around the coastline. I have already mentioned Dumfries, once the busiest west-coast port south of Glasgow; but there were other active little ports along the now silted-up Solway coastline, and numerous piers and quays up and down the east coast. Even more dependent on the sea was the ruggedly indented west coast, where paddle steamers brought cargoes and passengers from London or Glasgow to the Highlands and Islands throughout the year. As Alexander Smith recorded in his vividly evocative book *A Summer in Skye*, from which I have already quoted, in the early 1850s the Hebrides relied almost totally on the paddle steamer service of David MacBrayne for the necessities of life, and for the export of their cattle to the township markets. In the more doctrinally extreme 'Wee Free' parts of the Highlands the 'unco guid' (over-righteous) once held it blasphemy to sing the actual words of the psalms for rehearsal purposes. Secular parodies to fit the old tunes were therefore invented. A version of one of them, once widely popular in the West Highlands, ran:

The earth belongs unto the Lord
And all that it contains,
Except the Scottish Western Isles –
And they are all MacBrayne's.

The MacBrayne monopoly disappeared with the nationalisation of rail and road transport just after the end of the Second World War, though due to a nineteenth-century Act of Parliament designed to prevent one particularly thrusting railway company in Scotland from also owning a steamship company, the nationalised railway ships remained in the ownership of a subsidiary concern, The Caledonian Steam Packet Company. They, or at least their ungainly successors, are still theoretically

60

River Shiel, looking west towards Glen Shiel

Opposite:
Puffer at Craignure Pier, Mull

the property of a concern called Caledonian MacBrayne. Modern car ferries wearing the old names, but not the grace, beauty of line or personality of their predecessors, now sail out, mostly from Oban and Ullapool, to serve the Western Isles, carrying heavy goods and those tourists who want to bring their own cars with them, though many tourists, of course, prefer to fly into the larger islands and hire a car locally.

Oban, a holiday town clustering round a spectacular bay, has the tiny island of Lismore and the mountainy island of Mull to protect it to some extent from the full fury of the Atlantic. The town has developed beneath a hill crowned since 1897 with the unfinished outer wall of a great classical amphitheatre; a kind of Colosseum without a heart, intended to be a museum and outlook tower. It was the idea of a local banker and philanthropist who embarked on the project in 1897 to provide relief work for the unemployed. John Stewart MacCaig died, having spent £5,000, a huge sum in those days, but leaving the work incomplete, and known ever since, though affectionately, as 'MacCaig's Folly'.

The ship that lies at Oban pier in Dennis Hardley's photograph is not, however, based on Oban. Indeed, she has long since shed her middle-life connection with Caledonian MacBrayne. None other than the *Waverley*, the last sea-going paddle-steamer in the world, she was built in 1946 for the London and North Eastern Railway Company to replace the first *Waverley*, sunk off the beaches at Dunkirk in 1940 by German bombs.

Although for a time the second *Waverley* did ply on the Clyde under the nationalised colours, for the past decade or so she has been privately owned and managed. Decked once again in her original London and North Eastern Railway Company livery, she cruises in the Firth of Clyde throughout July and August, but during the earlier and later months of the season sails out of 'foreign' ports as far apart as Liverpool, Southend, London, and, as we see here, Oban.

Much larger paddle steamers once sailed out of Portpatrick, on the Mull of Galloway, the journey from this port to Donaghadee being the shortest sea crossing between Britain and Northern Ireland. Sir William Brereton, eventually a Parliamentary General in the Civil War, when still a young man made a remarkable journey to Scotland in 1634 and kept a pungent diary. Early in July he and his friends rode the four miles from St John, the village that stood on the site of what is now Stranraer, to Portpatrick, 'a foul winter way over the mossy moors.' There, he and his friends 'hired a boat of about ten ton for five horses; for this we paid £1 and conditioned that no more horses should come aboard, save only two or three of an Irish laird's, who then stayed for a passage, and carried his wife and three horses . . . We shipped our horses two hours before we went aboard. It was a most craggy, filthy passage, and very dangerous for horses to go in and out; a horse may easily be lamed, spoiled, and thrust into the sea; and when any horses land here, they are thrown into the sea and swim out.'

It must therefore have eased matters a little for travellers when a few years later, in 1662, a weekly mail service was inaugurated. The harbour, however, was exposed to frequent storms and the heaviness of the Atlantic swell. The pier, built in 1774, did little to cut down the number of cancelled voyages, so in 1821 a stronger harbour was designed and built by the famous engineer John Rennie. In 1838 the first steamboats came into service. Even the great stone blocks of Rennie's harbour could not withstand the fury of the elements, and in 1849 the service was abandoned. Stranraer, at the head of Loch Ryan, proved a more reliable shelter on the Scottish side, and Larne on the Irish side. Today, Portpatrick is a holiday resort, its harbour a convenient shelter for local fishing boats and a port of call for cabin cruisers.

Many Scottish harbours have long since lost their fishing fleets, giving tidal shelter only to a few small inshore boats plying to satisfy local needs. Such a place is Pennan, near Fraserburgh, a picturesque example of those one-time Scottish villages that clung to the coast beneath towering cliffs. Having difficult landward communications in bygone days, they had to stretch frail harbour arms into the North Sea to shelter their fishing fleets. A century ago a tiny village such as Pennan mustered about forty local boats.

Pittenweem, on the coast of Fife, and the widening shores of the Firth of Forth, has been rather luckier. Though once it was the base for more than fifty boats, a few do still regularly sail from its shallow harbour to brave the winds and sudden storms that blow up so quickly over the shallow North Sea. Many of Pittenweem's delightful traditional seventeenth- and eighteenth-century houses, with their red pantiled roofs and crow-stepped gables, have been restored, some by the National Trust for Scotland. It is now a popular place with passing tourists.

Herring fishing, since time immemorial a traditional Scottish industry, went into decline during the First World War when the market for salted herring, packed in locally made barrels and despatched to Russia and Germany disappeared. It was a market only partially recovered after the

Beach at Seilebost, Harris

*Eigg and Rhum from
Ardnamurchan*

Opposite:
P.S. Waverley, *the last sea-going
paddle-steamer, at Oban*

Armistice. In pre-war days and throughout the 'Thirties it was steam
drifters that netted the once-plentiful herring, anchoring sixty miles or
so from port and paying out a trailing mile of net.

The white fish steam trawlers, away for a week at a time, sailed from
the major ports; Grimsby and Hull in England, and Peterhead and
Aberdeen in Scotland.

A few of the steam drifters survived the Second World War, though
not for long. Even the diesel-driven smaller boats which replaced them
found the old market impossible to recapture after the return of peace in
1946. In recent years the absence of an internationally agreed conservation
policy, and the incursion into Scottish waters of foreign ships, including
Eastern bloc factory ships, are blamed for the further decline of the market
– though, to be fair, some Scots fishermen admit that they are glad enough
to sell to the foreigners when prices are poor on the home market.

Though a major fishing centre, Aberdeen was also for long a passenger
harbour, maintaining a regular service to and from London until 1939
and providing an important port of call for the fleet of ships plying
between Leith and Orkney and Shetland. Unlike the harbour fronts of
most sea-faring places Aberdeen harbour, though reaching almost into
the heart of the city, has never been an unsalubrious area. Its grey granite
buildings flecked with mica flash in the glinting sunlight as cleanly as in
the central shopping street of the city.

68

Portpatrick Harbour

Opposite:
Oban at night

Some find the glittering greyness of granite an unsympathetic though durable material. The people who inhabit this city largely built of granite are hard-headed in business and, until you get to know them, as dour-seeming as their cold environment; the butt, indeed, of countless jokes about meanness. The fact is that the Aberdeen joke industry was mainly local, and a profitable one at that.

In spite of Aberdonian jokes, beyond all doubt Aberdeen is, and always has been, a singularly industrious city. Nowadays it is the northern centre of the North Sea oil business, its airport a constant shuttle of planes linking it with other continents, and sea-going helicopters flying to and from the distant oil rigs. From its harbour, in place of the former passenger steamers, boats that look like floating lorries shuttle backwards and forwards to and from the rigs, carrying the heavier goods and stores.

To be in Aberdeen today is to experience a thrill of prosperity such as must once have nerved Glasgow, the largest of Scotland's cities but now shrinking in decline as the profitability of its heavy industries, coal mines and the iron and steel-making capacities on which its prosperity once depended recedes further and further into history. By contrast, Aberdeen has become increasingly cosmopolitan, the accents of Texas and the language of Norway frequently to be heard in its shopping streets. Not so long ago I looked into the window of a shop inside an Aberdeen hotel. The goods were priced first in American dollars, second in Norwegian kroner, and third in sterling! The times have long gone when an

Aberdonian could say with any practical justification: 'A day oot o' Aiberdeen's a day oot o'life!'

Whether in Aberdeen or Oban, Pennan or Pittenweem, there is a fascination in watching the movement of ships and boats; a fascination that has fired the blood of the Scots for centuries. Inland, and every bit as deep-rooted as the seafaring folk, are the farmers; men long familiar with the speak of the good earth. The city dwellers have antennae perhaps less responsive to the seasons. Many of them care probably as little for the domestic habits of the skylark as for the sex-life of the skate. Yet in a country with a coastline as serrated by the ocean as is that of Scotland, with innumerable long sea lochs reaching deep into the hills, tumbling rivers relentlessly wearing away even its most ancient and durable mountains, and countless freshwater lochs and lochans, the never very distant presence of the sea, the movement of water and the ways in which we harness it are matters of endless fascination.

Opposite:
Pittenweem Harbour, Fife

Pennan Harbour, near New Aberdour

72

Aberdeen Harbour

74

Evening sun, Loch Duich

76

6

Innumerable lochs and one natural lake – the Lake of Menteith – stare upwards to skies from which they receive their energy. On a clear day it is impossible to fly over Scotland without being aware of the glint of water caught in the slanting sunshine. Somewhere, perhaps, hidden among the less important national statistics, a record exists enumerating and categorising Scotland's lochs into sea lochs, freshwater lochs and mere lochans. I have never searched for it. Neither have I made such a count myself, nor met anyone who systematically 'logs' lochs, as mountaineers do Munros, as mountains higher than three thousand feet are called.

The selection of lochs that Dennis Hardley's camera has captured is, on the whole, a representative one. There are the lonely lochs still hardly ever visited by man because of their inaccessibility. But loneliness and the grandeur its mountainy barriers so often suggest are by no means always out of human reach. Of the sea lochs of the Western Highlands, none is more lovely than Loch Duich, which deflects from the head of Loch Alsh, in the area once known as Wester Ross, and runs along the Kintail shore. Near its head loom the Five Sisters of Kintail (of which there are actually six, though only five are to be seen on the skyline from below): Sgurr nan Spainteach, 3,129 feet high, Sgurr na Ciste Duibh, 3,370 feet, Sgurr Fhuaran, 3,505 feet, Sgurr na Carnach, 3,270 feet, Sgurr nan Saighead, 2,987 feet, and Sgurr na Moraich, 2,870 feet high. The road to Strathappin runs along the northern coast of the loch, that to Glenshiel along the southern. The compiler of the last descriptive *Ordnance Gazetteer of Scotland*, which appeared in 1901 and must therefore presumably have been written during the final years of Queen Victoria's reign, thought that from any approach, 'a scene gradually unfolds which it is impossible to describe.' The anonymous writer then went on to attempt the impossible. 'Mountains of universal magnitude', he wrote, 'grouped together in the sublimest manner, with wood and water, seas and bens intermingled, present a prospect seldom surpassed in wild beauty, and equally interesting and astonishing in the storms of winter and the calm serenity of summer.' The phrases 'wild beauty' and 'astonishing' would almost certainly still run from the pen of a topographical writer attempting a similar task today. The countryside round the village of Kintail is Mackenzie and Macrae territory, the Clan Macrae having come to the district in the fourteenth century to serve the more powerful Mackenzies, later earls of Seaforth, 'as fighting men, earning the nickname of the "Mackenzies' shirt of mail".'

The Great Glen, that natural fault, or long fracture, that divides Scotland from south east to north west, is filled by four interlinked lochs: Loch Ness, Loch Oich, Loch Lochy and Loch Linnhe, the last running into the Sound of Mull and the Firth of Lorne. All were connected and made navigable by the construction of the Caledonian Canal. James Watt, the practical perfector of the steam engine, drew up plans as early as 1773, but on grounds of cost nothing was done until 1803 when the great engineer Thomas Telford began the canal, though the project was not fully completed until 1847. The poet Robert Southey accompanied Telford on a tour of inspection in 1819, and was much impressed by the construction work.

'Such an extent of masonry, upon such a scale, I had never before beheld, each of the Locks being 180 feet in length. It was a most impressive

Fort Augustus, Loch Ness

and memorable scene. Men, horses and machines at work: digging, walling and puddling going on, men wheeling barrows, horses drawing stores along the railways. The great steam engine was at rest, having done its work. It threw out 160 hogsheads a minute; and two smaller engines (large ones they would have been considered anywhere else) were also needed while the excavation of the lower docks was going on; for they dug 24 feet below the surface of the water in the river, and the water filtered thro' open gravel. The dredging machine was in action, revolving round and round, and bringing up at every turn matter which had never before been brought to the air and light.'

The Caledonian Canal was much used by small vessels, mainly fishing boats, anxious to avoid the storms of the Pentland Firth, and by seasonal passenger steamers, until the outbreak of the Second World War. Nowadays, unfortunately, it can only be used in parts by small pleasure craft, since like all canals, it poses costly maintenance problems. Two locks link Loch Oich and Loch Lochy, the height of which was artificially raised by twelve feet by the closing of its effluence into the River Lochy.

Loch Linnhe, looked at across the narrows of the Corran ferry towards the hills of Ardgour, is one of the loveliest of Scotland's sea lochs. It stretches from Corpach, near Fort William, to the Sound of Mull. Into it flow Loch Eil, at its head; the fiercely tidal narrow-necked Loch Leven, near Ballachulish; Loch Creran, to the north of Benderloch; and Loch Etive to the south. The island of Lismore lies in its lower reaches.

Originally christianised by Saint Moluag, who was probably a contemporary of Saint Columba but of British origin, Lismore achieved literary fame by the discovery at the end of the nineteenth century of *The Book of the Dean of Lismore* (d.1533), an anthology of Gaelic poems which appeared to include the fragments from which James Macpherson might have worked up his famous eighteenth-century Ossianic poems in English.

Like so many Highland lochs, including those in the Great Glen, Loch Awe, twenty-two miles long but rarely more than a mile wide, runs north east to south west. Thought by William Gilpin, the 'inventor' of the theory of the picturesque, to be 'one of the grandest lakes in Scotland', it lies in the heart of Argyll, and was at one time entirely dominated by the Clan Campbell, providing a kind of protective moat against attack in the north of their territory as the sea arm of Loch Fyne did in the south. Oddly enough, Loch Awe flows not into the sea at its south end, by Ford, but more circuitously; to the north through Loch Etive. Loch Awe has several islands, among them Kilchurn, as already mentioned merely marsh-girt, and, also with its ruined keep, Innis Chonell, once maintained for the Campbells by the MacArthurs. Now, the only 'warfare' carried on is against the salmon and the trout, trout-fishing here beginning in March, earlier than anywhere else in Scotland.

The mountain of Ben Lui towers above the gaunt skeleton of Kilchurn Castle, though the dominating peak is that most strongly associated with the Campbells, Ben Cruachan. It gives its name to the Cruachan hydro-electric scheme, at the north-west end of the loch. This scheme, constructed by the North of Scotland Hydro-Electric Board in 1965, is one of many that have harnessed Highland waters in post-Second World War days. This one was, indeed, the Board's first pump storage scheme, and incorporates a reversible turbine, the first of its kind to be brought into use anywhere in the world.

One other sea loch features in this anthology, Loch Goil. Stand yourself above the Firth of Clyde at the resort and railhead of Gourock, or on Lyle Hill, behind Greenock, its industrial neighbour, and one of the most beautiful vistas in Europe lies open before you. To the north, across the widened estuary, are the Cowal Hills, once the barrier between Highlands and Lowlands. Around 1850, the historian Robert Chambers could write comfortably: 'But a few miles off across the Firth of Clyde, the untameable Highland territory stretches away into Alpine solitudes of the wildest character; so that it is possible to sit in a Greenock drawing-room amidst a scene of refinement not surpassed, and of industry unexampled in Scotland, with the cultivated Lowlands at your back, and let the imagination follow the eye into a blue distance where things still exhibit nearly the same moral aspect as they did a thousand years ago. It is said that when Rob Roy haunted the opposite coasts of Dumbartonshire, he found it very convenient to sail across and make a selection from the goods displayed in the Greenock fairs; on which occasion the ellwands and staves of civilisation would come into collision with the broadswords and dirks of savage warfare in such a style as might have served to show the extremely slight hold which the law had as yet taken of certain parts of our country.'

Since the days of Robert Chambers, let alone those of Rob Roy, the celebrated hero of one of Sir Walter Scott's most famous novels, much has changed. The coming of the steamboat resulted in the growth of the Gaelic-speaking clachan of Dunoon into a holiday town, and throughout the second half of the nineteenth century the development of ornate

Loch Lochy, Invernessshire

81

Right:
Portsonachan, Loch Awe, and
Ben Cruachan

Loch Kanaird, from Ardmair

villas and the hamlets of the estuary's northern coastline. Greenock itself was to retain much of the prosperity it already held in Chambers' day, through shipbuilding and engineering, sugar refining and other industries, which flourished until post-Second World War days; and then to feel again, as during the hungry 'Thirties, the sharp edge of recession. The fleet of colourful paddle-steamers and turbines that once served such estuarial watering-places as Kirn, Dunoon, Innellan and Rothesay, was to give place to squatly ugly car ferries.

What has remained unchanged is that glorious vista, which leads the eye over the water to the north of the Holy Loch – now, ironically, the Clyde base of the American 'Polaris' submarines! – and Loch Long, never unduly spoiled by its use over several decades as a testing ground for naval torpedo engines. Branching north out of Loch Long, its mouth almost opposite a well-concealed oil terminal connected by pipe-line across Scotland to a refinery at Grangemouth, on the Forth, is Loch Goil. Lochgoilhead, at the head of the loch, was once an exclusive Clyde watering place served by a daily steamer service. Now, it is surrounded by the woodlands of Argyll National Forest Park. On the west side of the loch stands Carrick Castle, a fifteenth-century tower unroofed but reasonably intact, and once a royal stronghold, though occupied by the Earls of Argyll as hereditary keepers.

Finally, there are three of what might be termed the 'Glasgow lochs', in that they are within easy access of that city; indeed, more or less within Glasgow's commuter belt, although they have managed to preserve their natural magnificence nonetheless.

Two of them – Loch Ard, near Aberfoyle, and Loch Katrine, in the Trossachs – are in what used to be known as the Perthshire Highlands, greener and less rugged than the Western Highlands. Loch Ard, which lies in the course of the northern head-stream of the River Forth, has been vividly described by Sir Walter Scott in *Rob Roy*: 'High hills, rocks and banks, waving with natural forests of birch and oak, framed the borders of this enchanting sheet of water; and as their leaves rustled to the wind and twinkled in the sun, gave to the depth of solitude a sort of life and vivacity . . . . The road now suddenly emerged, and, winding close by the margin of the loch, afforded us a full view of its spacious mirror, which reflected in still magnificence the high dark heathy mountains, huge grey rocks, and shaggy banks by which it is encircled.' In a wooded ravine by the double waterfall of Ledard, near the head of the loch, Scott, in *Waverley*, his first novel, had the hero, Captain Waverley, meet the heroine, Flora MacIvor. Also near the head of the loch are the ruins of a castle built by Murdoch, Duke of Albany and Regent of Scotland. Tradition has it that it was to this stronghold he fled in 1425, and from which he was seized and taken to his execution at Stirling.

Scott's association with Loch Katrine is even stronger, for it forms the setting for his poem *The Lady of the Lake*. He visited Loch Katrine on several occasions between 1790 and 1809, the year before the publication of his poem. Though the raising of the level of the loch by seventeen feet to accommodate the submerged aqueduct constructed between 1856 and 1859 for Glasgow's waterworks (opened on 14 October 1859) swamped the Silver Strand, opposite Ellen's Isle, the loveliness of the loch has not otherwise been harmed by its domestic function. Since 1900, an elegant yacht-like steamship, now the oldest surviving Scottish pleasure-boat still in service, has sailed from the Trossachs end of the loch to Stronachlachar at its head.

Overleaf:
The Firth of Clyde, from above Gourock

83

*Esplanade Fountain, Rothesay,
Bute*

*Opposite:
Loch Ard, near Aberfoyle*

The Wordsworths, along with Coleridge, also visited Loch Katrine. While the brother and sister rowed down it, Coleridge rested in a hut. Wrote Dorothy: 'After turning a rocky point we came to a bay closed in by rocks and steep woods, chiefly of full-grown birch . . . . After we had left this bay we saw before us a long reach of woods and rocks and rocky points, that promised other bays more beautiful than what we had passed . . . . The second bay we came to differed from the rest; the hills retired a space from the lake, leaving a few level fields between, on which was a cottage embosomed in trees: the bay was defended by rocks at each end, and the hills behind made a shelter for the cottage, the only dwelling, I believe, except one, on this side of Loch Kettering.

'We now came to steeps that rose directly from the lake, and passed by a place called in the Gaelic the Den of the Ghosts (Goblins' Cave), which reminded us of Lodore; it is a rock, or mass of rock, with a stream of large black stones like the naked or dried-up bed of a torrent down the side of it; birch-trees start out of the rock in every direction, and cover the hill above, further than we could see. The water of the lake below was very deep, black and calm. Our delight increased as we advanced, till we came to the termination of the lake, seeing where the river issues out of it through a chasm between the hills . . . . It was in entire solitude; and all that we beheld was the perfection of loveliness and beauty.'

So, finally, to Loch Lomond, the queen of all the Scottish lochs and the longest inland waterway in Britain. Twenty-four miles long, it ranges

in breadth from about five miles at the Lowland end, where Balloch is a mere seventeen miles from the heart of Glasgow, to three-quarters-of-a-mile near Tarbet, where it plunges into the Highland mountains. The poet Southey, who visited it in 1819, counted thirty-six islands, including what he called the 'mere dots'. The largest is Inchmurrin, which contains an old castle that was a seat of the earls of Lennox, an hotel and several houses, some of the occupants of which daily commute, first by motor-boat to the mainland, and then by road to Glasgow. Inchcailliach, the 'women's island', has the ruins of a nunnery on it, and was the burial place of the MacGregors. Five islands, including Inchcailliach and Clairinch, as well as part of the shore and its marshy hinterland, now form a Nature Reserve.

Once, in geological time, Loch Lomond was linked to the Clyde, but the short River Leven now connects it with that waterway, flowing past Dumbarton Rock on its course. Many of the early paddle-steamers which carried supplies to the villages and hamlets along the 'bonnie, bonnie banks of Loch Lomond', and in summer took sightseers and tourists aboard – in 1847, the famous Danish story-teller Hans Andersen among them – were built on the Clyde and floated up the Leven. The last but one got stuck, however, and remained stranded in the Leven for several months. The only survivor of the fleet, *The Maid of the Loch*, the last paddle-steamer to be built in Britain, was constructed in a Clydeside yard in 1955, taken to pieces, conveyed in sections to Balloch, at the foot of the loch, and there reassembled. In 1982, British Rail sold her to private owners. At the moment of writing her fate is uncertain, although her new owners have announced plans to convert her into a weekday quality restaurant, and sail her at weekends during the summer season, leaving the daily shorter trips to be undertaken by the screw-steamer *Countess Fiona*, herself a veteran since, as the *Countess of Breadalbane*, she first went into service on Loch Awe in 1936.

Loch Lomond carries many small private pleasure craft, but because of the speed with which winds can funnel through the mountains, it is a stretch of water that must always be treated with respect and care, as Mendelssohn found out when, in 1829, he and his friend, the poet and diplomat Karl Klingemann, pushed off from its shores.

'The day before yesterday, on Loch Lomond, we were sitting in a small rowing boat and were going to cross to the opposite shore, invited by a gleaming light, when there came a sudden tremendous gust of wind from the mountains. The boat began to see-saw so fearfully that I caught up my cloak and got ready to swim. All our things were thrown topsy-turvy, and Klingemann anxiously called to me, "Look sharp, look sharp!" But with our usual good luck we got safely through.'

The best encomium of all, however, comes from the pen of the French geologist, B. Faujas St Fond, who came to Scotland in 1778, mainly to see the basaltic island of Staffa.

'The superb Loch Lomond', he rhapsodised; 'the fine sunlight that gilded its waters, the silvery rocks that skirted its shores, the flowery and verdant mosses, the black oxen, the white sheep, the shepherds beneath the pines, the perfume of the tea poured into cups that had been given by kindness, and received with gratitude, will never be effaced from my memory, and make me cherish the desire not to die before seeing Tarbet. I shall often dream of Tarbet, even in the midst of lovely Italy with its oranges, its myrtles, its laurels, and its jessamines.'

Superb it remains to this day, in all weathers and moods.

P.S. Maid of the Loch *at Inversnaid, Loch Lomond*

90

7

Opposite:
The Kibble Palace, the Botanic
Gardens, Glasgow

Overleaf:
Edinburgh Castle from the Calton
Hill

Glasgow has some claim to be included in an album entitled *Unknown Scotland*, for since the decline of its industrial power, when it was dubbed 'The Second City of the Empire' – a title it lost, numerically, to Birmingham about 1938 – the widely projected image of itself has been one compounded of troubled industrial relationships, murderous violence and seething drunkenness. Like all large industrial cities in the transitional process of contracting and adapting to new purposes, the old heavy industry-based ones having gone, it has its share of these vices. But the days depicted in MacArthur's novel of the Gorbals *No Mean City* have long since vanished, as certainly as the crumbled fabric of that once-infamous slum.

Just as Edinburgh, along with its historic Old Town, has in its New Town – built, roughly speaking, between 1768 and 1848 – the finest and most extensive piece of Georgian town planning in Europe, so Glasgow possesses the finest Victorian urban heritage of buildings in Britain, a heritage it has come increasingly to care about and look after. Those who explore Scotland always visit Edinburgh, the Capital. Too often they miss out Glasgow, and therefore fail to enjoy what is still a visually stimulating experience. Furthermore, not only is Glasgow the home of Scottish Opera and the Scottish National Orchestra, among other cultural credits; it also possesses the Burrell Gallery, in the grounds of William Adam's Pollock House, a magnificent parkland mansion in the bounds of the city, and the Burrell Collection, one of the most varied and perceptively gathered assemblages of pictures and *objets d'art* to be found in Northern Europe.

Dennis Hardley has given only token representation to Scotland's three largest cities. Since one impact of this book may very well be to entice travellers from England, the rest of Europe and, indeed, the world to visit Scotland, Europe's knuckle-end, I can only urge them not only to use Edinburgh, Aberdeen and Glasgow as nodal points for excursions to some of the scenes depicted in these pages, but also to explore the delights the cities themselves have to offer.

Delight! Sooner or later the word had to come in, after the experience of so much of the pictorial variety displayed in these pages. What better way to leave you, as you close for a while the covers of this book, than with two rhetorical questions propounded by Sir Walter Scott and, to both of which, were it possible, I, for one, would give an unqualified affirmative:

'What is this life, if it be not mixed with some delight? And what delight is more pleasing than to see the fashions and manners of unknown places?'